Robby Just Wants to Help

A Fengtastic Tale About Learning and AI

Tiankai Feng

Technics Publications

TECHNICS PUBLICATIONS

115 Linda Vista, Sedona, AZ 86336 USA

https://www.TechnicsPub.com
Edited by Steve Hoberman

Cover design by Lorena Molinari
Author photo by Yan Li

First Printing 2026

ISBN, print ed. 9798898160708

Library of Congress Control Number: 2026934720

For Sky and Cloud, who teach me something new every day—

and for Yan, my best friend, partner,

and mother of our beautiful children.

Sky and Cloud are two brothers who love each other very much, even if they fight sometimes, especially when they're competing in games. Sky is the older brother who loves reading and drawing. Cloud loves playing football and climbing on everything he can find. Together, they love building LEGO™ towers, racing in Mario Kart, and most of all, experimenting with new things!

One evening, Dad came home with a surprise. It was a little metallic robot with round glowing eyes and tiny wheels for feet.

“This is Robby,” Dad said. “He’s going to help us around the house. But first, you’ll need to teach him how—otherwise things might go a bit wonky!”

“Robby learns by looking at lots of examples,” Dad explained. “If you show him a hundred pictures of apples, he spots the pattern, like the round shape with a stem on top, and the colors of red or green. Then he can recognize new apples he’s never seen!

We call this *artificial intelligence* because he imitates how humans think, but he’s not actually human.”

The boys asked Robby to clean their messy room. “CLEANING. MODE. ACTIVATED,” Robby announced. But when they came back, Robby had taken apart their bookshelf, desk, and bunk bed. Robbie had sorted all of the furniture pieces into neat little piles!

"You told Robby to clean, but not what NOT to do," Dad explained. "We call these limits *guardrails*, just like the bumpers in bowling that keep the ball out of the gutter. Robby needs to know his boundaries!" The boys added a new rule: "Do NOT take apart furniture. Ever." Robby beeped apologetically, his eyes turning a sorry purple.

3+4 = 7
5+8 = 10
13-7 = 5
3×5 = 20
33+8=40

Sky was tired after school and asked Robby to help with his maths homework. He showed Robby all his old worksheets so Robby could learn. But when Sky got his homework back, half was right and half was wrong. Robbie made the exact same mistakes Sky always made!

A+

"Nobody told Robby which answers were correct and which were mistakes," Dad said. "So he learned both! What was missing is *labeling*. Labeling is like putting green stickers on good answers and red stickers on wrong ones. Without labels, Robby thinks everything is right, even the mistakes."

Cloud looked up from his building blocks. "When I go to big school, I'm putting stickers on everything!"

The boys asked Robby to decorate for the Lunar New Year. It's the Year of the Dragon!

But when they checked, Robby had hung up pictures of moons and fireworks everywhere. No red lanterns. No dragons. No lucky decorations!

"LUNAR. MEANS. MOON," Robby explained, confused.

福

“Robby does not know about traditions,” Dad explained. “The red color for luck, the lanterns, and the zodiac animals. He just guessed from the words.” The boys spent the afternoon showing Robby pictures of real Lunar New Year celebrations.

“Now I understand!” Robby chirped happily. “RED. DRAGONS. FAMILY. TOGETHER.”

Mustard

Sky asked Robby for Mom's special cookie recipe. Robby answered confidently: "TWO CUPS OF FLOUR, ONE CUP OF SUGAR, HALF A CUP OF MUSTARD, THREE PICKLES, AND A SPOONFUL OF GLITTER."

Cloud burst out laughing. "PICKLES? GLITTER?"

When they told Mom, she laughed so hard she had to sit down. "My cookies have chocolate chips—not pickles!"

Recipe:
chips 'n' screws
spicy pickles
3 eggs
sugar + oil

"When Robby doesn't know something, he sometimes makes things up instead of saying 'I don't know,'" Dad explained. "We call this *hallucinating*. Hallucinating is imagining things that aren't there. Just because Robby sounds sure doesn't mean he's right. Always check!"

Robby's eyes turned a sheepish pink. "I. WILL. TRY. TO. SAY. WHEN. I. DO. NOT. KNOW."

“For Mom’s birthday, the boys asked Robby to design her a dress. They gave him old photos from before they were born. Robby’s design had huge puffy sleeves, an old-fashioned pattern, and was much too small!

Mum hugged them kindly. “How sweet of you to try!”

SHOPPINE
CENTER

"Those photos were twenty years old," Dad explained. "People change! Fashion changes! If you give Robby old information, he'll give you old results."

Cloud nodded. "It's like using a treasure map from a hundred years ago—all the streets have changed!"

ZRRRR....

The boys got into a habit of asking Robby everything.

"What time is it?" "Is it raining?" "Where's my sock?"

One afternoon, Robby's voice slowed, his eyes flickered, and he made a sad whirring sound...then shut down completely.

"ROBBY!" the boys cried.

"Every question uses electricity," Dad said, plugging Robby in to charge. "Asking Robby uses ten times more energy than looking something up yourself. One question is small, but millions of questions add up to using as much electricity as a whole city!"

Cloud looked at the clock on the wall. "I could have just...looked myself."

"Exactly! Not everything needs a robot."

100

When Robby woke up, his eyes glowed a grateful green.

"THANK. YOU. FOR. LETTING. ME. REST."

Over the following weeks, Sky and Cloud became experts at working with Robby.

They learned to give him clear instructions AND clear boundaries. They labeled things so he knew right from wrong. They gave him all the right information—and made sure it wasn't outdated!

They also learned to check Robby's answers—especially when he sounded too sure. And they only asked for his help when they really needed it, saving his energy for the tricky problems.

One quiet evening, Sky asked, “Dad, will robots ever be as smart as people?”

Dad thought carefully. “Robby can remember more facts than any human and work much faster. But there’s something special about humans that Robby will never have.”

"All the things you know but have never said out loud," Dad continued. "The way you know Mom is sad even when she says she's fine. The way you can tell a joke might hurt someone's feelings. The way you can imagine something completely new."

Dad tapped his head. “There’s knowledge in here we can’t put into words. That’s why robots will always need humans to guide them.”

“So, we’re like Robby’s teachers?” Cloud asked.

“And his partners. You help each other.”

Robby whirred happily. “THANK. YOU. FOR. TEACHING. ME.”

That night, as the boys lay in bed, they imagined how robots might help people in the future.

Sky pictured doctors with robot assistants, searching through thousands of medical books in seconds to help sick patients get better.

Cloud imagined firefighters with brave robot helpers, zooming into burning buildings to rescue people trapped inside.

They both dreamed of chefs with robot sous chefs, chopping vegetables at lightning speed while the human chef taste-tested the soup and added the perfect sprinkle of seasoning.

“The robots do the hard work,” Cloud murmured sleepily, “and the humans make sure it’s done right.”

“Partners,” Sky agreed.

79...

Downstairs, Robby was charging quietly, his eyes glowing a soft, peaceful blue. He was just a machine—but with Sky and Cloud to teach him, who knew what they might accomplish together?

The future was bright. And it belonged to humans and their robot friends, working side by side.

The End

Artificial Intelligence
Robot
Training Data
Guardrails
Labeling
Hallucination
Energy

Glossary for Grown-Ups

Artificial Intelligence (AI): Computer systems designed to perform tasks that typically require human intelligence, such as recognising patterns, making decisions, and understanding language.

Robot: A machine that can carry out actions automatically, often guided by AI or programmed instructions—Robby is a robot powered by AI.

Training Data: Examples that teach AI to spot patterns.

Guardrails: Rules that tell AI what NOT to do.

Labeling: Marking information as right or wrong so AI can tell the difference.

Hallucination: When AI makes something up instead of saying "I don't know."

Energy: AI uses lots of electricity—save it for when you really need it!

About the Author

Tiankai Feng is a Data & AI leader by day, a musician by night, and an optimist at heart. He believes in keeping humans at the center of our AI future.

Sky and Cloud are his two sons, whose curiosity and endless questions inspired this story.

This is Tiankai's first *fengtastic tale*.

www.ingramcontent.com/pod-product-compliance
Lightning Source LLC
LaVergne TN
LVHW070857210926
848482LV00016B/965

9798898160708